Alphabet affirmationZ

Colin McLeod Green

BALBOA.PRESS

A DIVISION OF HAY HOUSE

Balboa Press books may be ordered through booksellers or by contacting:

Balboa Press
A Division of Hay House
1663 Liberty Drive
Bloomington, IN 47403
www.balboapress.com
844-682-1282

ISBN: 978-1-9822-4577-1 (sc)

Library of Congress Control Number: 2020906159

Print information available on the last page.

Balboa Press rev. date: 11/23/2020

*This coloring book is dedicated to all those who strive
to find their inner peace through self-love.*

A beAuty	This word was the original motivation behind the book. It reminds us to see the beauty all around.	**N** eNergy	There is energy in everything... What colors describe your personal energy?
B viBration	A pattern that is felt rather than seen, connecting everything to everything... What color is your vibration today?	**O** cOmpassion	A beautiful, healing word... and a reminder to have compassion toward yourself and others.
C presenCe	Many patterns and symbols can inspire presence. This particular design was inspired by the stone Larimar.	**P** emPathy	The genuine emotional connection to another living soul... I encourage you to ponder this...
D meDitate	This piece inspires me to see the space between moments... That space where stillness happens.	**Q** tranQuil	In Design, horizontal lines evoke a sense of calm and tranquility.
E brEathe	Inhale and Exhale. We can heal ourselves in these micro-moments. Just Breathe...	**R** gRatitude	O, how many ways there are to express our gratitude... How do you express your feelings of gratitude?
F mindFul	Be mindful of the opening at the top of this page... There you will find the opening to a labyrinth.	**S** enviSion	Where imagination dances and dreams grow... visualizing all possibility.
G orGanic	For me, organic means honoring nature and seeing the connection in every aspect of life... What does it mean to you?	**T** manTra	A lovely repetitive practice to help keep us grounded.
H exHale	Bring your focus to the exhale... This represents letting go, offering space for new things.	**U** trUth	The truth is in our present moment... Follow the labyrinth... stay present.
I belIeve	Believing in myself, even to the smallest degree, has brought incredible moments that inspire me to smile out loud...	**V** ferVor	Share your passion, inspire excitement, and achieve great things...
J enJoyment	I find my enjoyment in various forms of art, nature and music. Where do you find your enjoyment?	**W** empoWer	How can we collaborate to empower each other...? What empowers you?
K chaKras	Bring your awareness to these wheels of energy. When aligned, we can feel balanced & peaceful.	**X** eXpand	Just like the universe, we are in a constant flow of expansion and retraction...
L pLayful	How often do we forget to tap in to that inner child and play? Go ahead... dance, blow bubbles, be playful!	**Y** rhYthm	Identify the rhythm for your healing, your joy, your life...
M adMire	What aspects in yourself do you admire?	**Z** Zen	Release your laser focus on life and find your Zen.

Coloring Book

Scratch Page

Scratch Page

Scratch Page

Scratch Page

Scratch Page

Scratch Page

Scratch Page

Scratch Page

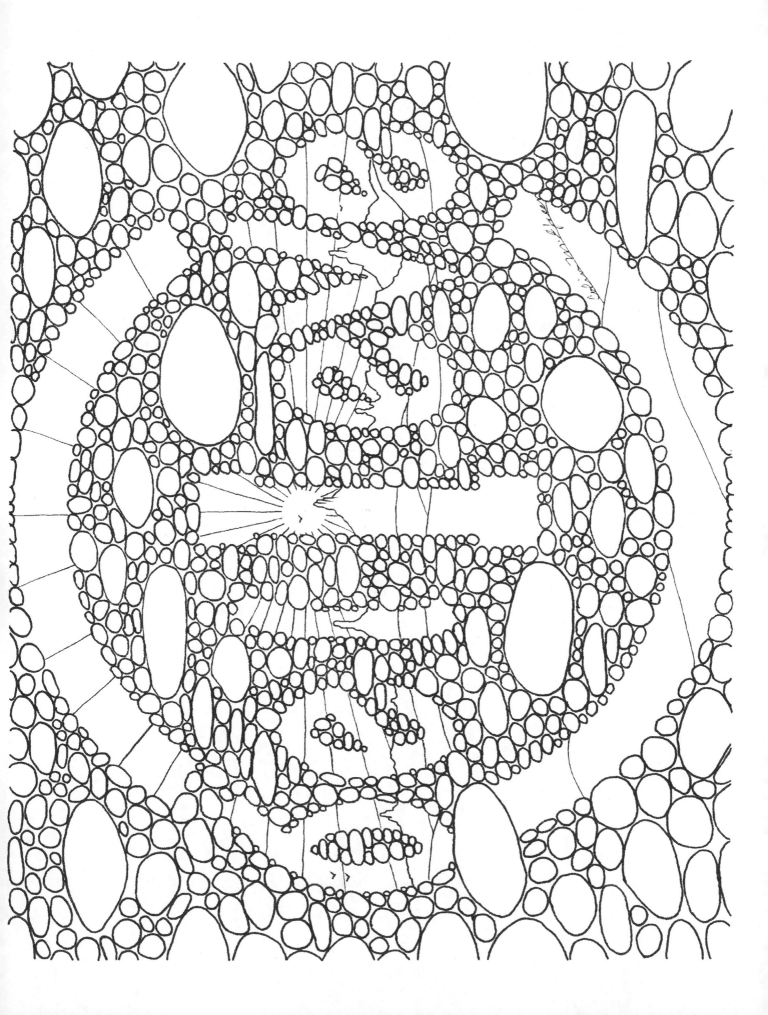

Scratch Page

Scratch Page

Scratch Page

Scratch Page

Scratch Page

Scratch Page

Scratch Page

Scratch Page

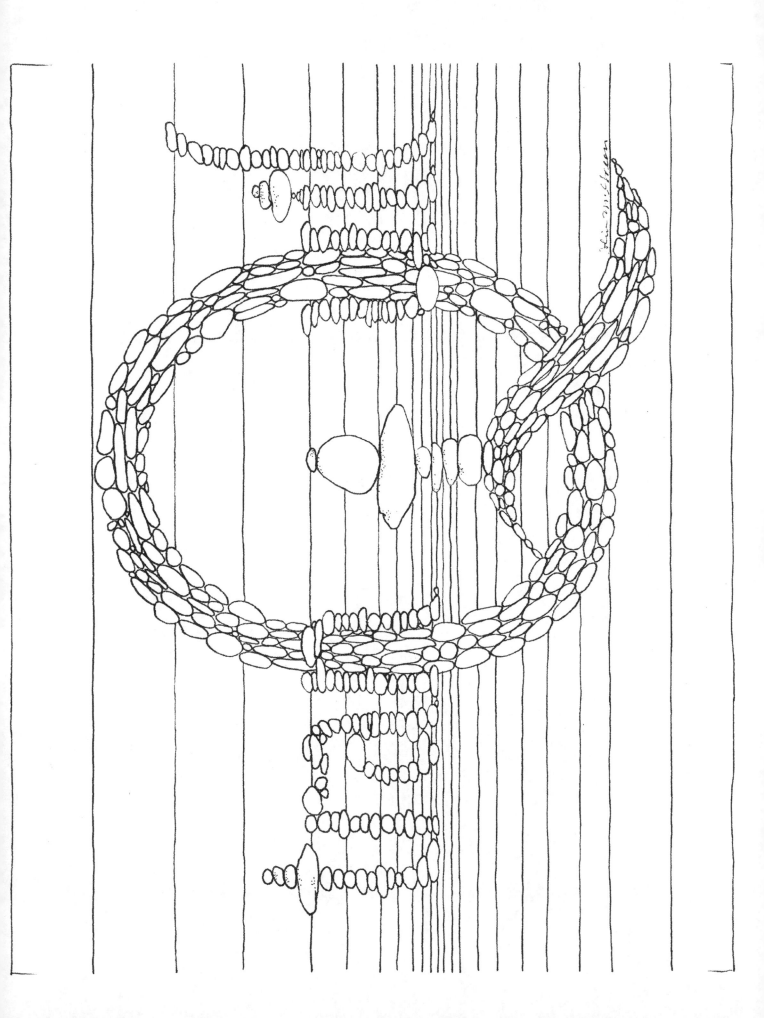

Scratch Page

Scratch Page

Scratch Page

Scratch Page

Scratch Page

Scratch Page

Scratch Page

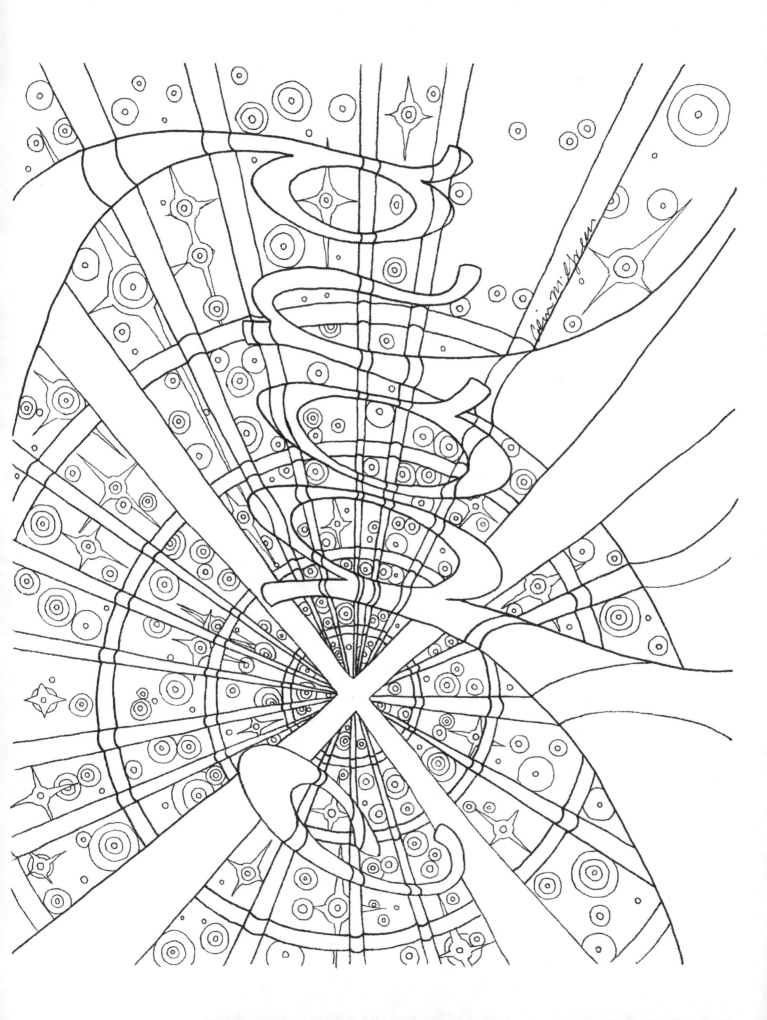

Scratch Page

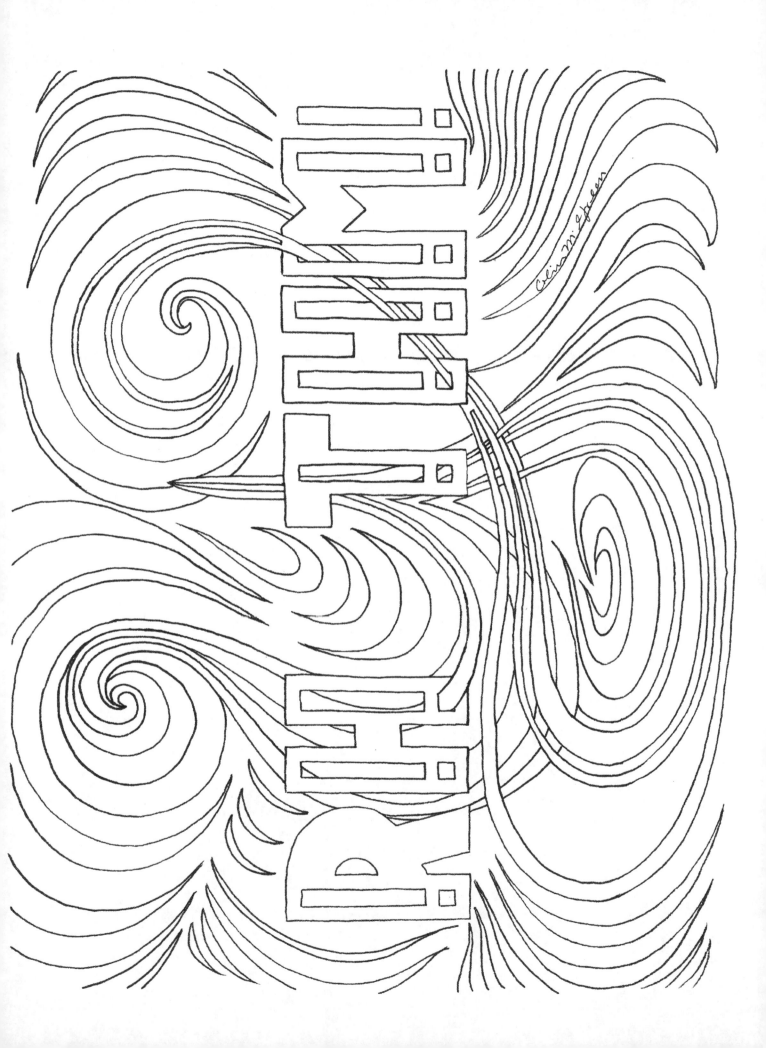

Scratch Page

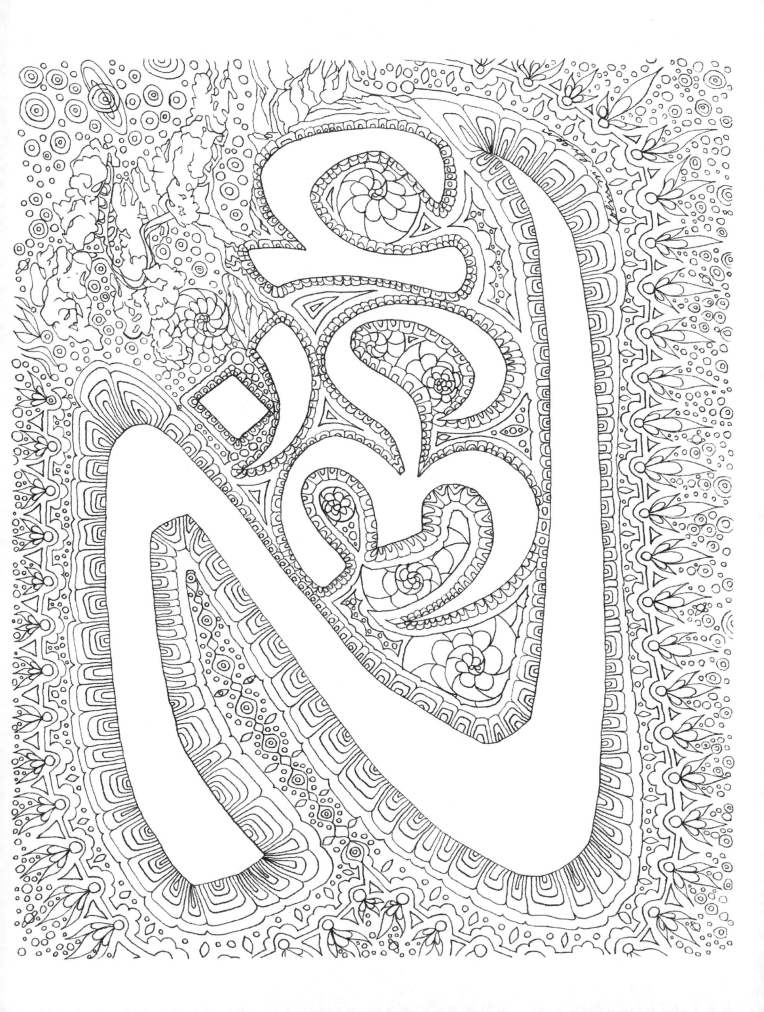

Scratch Page

Printed in the United States
By Bookmasters